The Might

MW00572836

Contents

Which Tool?

Sonia has a problem. She's helping her mother paint her bedroom. Sonia can hardly wait to get started.

Her first job is to open the can of paint. She tries to pull the lid off, but she can't do it. The lid is sealed tight.

Sonia takes the can downstairs to the workshop where the tools are. But there are so many tools, and they all look so different, Sonia doesn't know which one to use.

Which tool will help Sonia lift the lid?

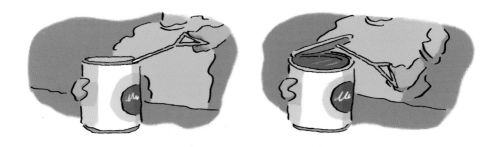

Sonia uses this tool to open the can of paint. Without it, she wouldn't be able to lift the lid.

This tool is a lever. A lever can help you lift or move objects. It makes work—such as opening a can of paint—a lot easier!

Now Sonia and her mom can get started painting her bedroom.

Pushing and Pulling

When Sonia wanted to open the paint can, she tried to pull the lid up. To move things, you have to push or pull them. These pushing and pulling movements are called **forces**.

Look around—there are moving things everywhere. You are moving, trucks and cars are moving, bikes are moving, doors are opening and closing, drawers are sliding in and out, lids are coming off. All of these movements use force—pushing and pulling.

When you kick a soccer ball, you're using a pushing force.

When you move your wagon filled with things, you're using a pulling force.

You need pushes and pulls to make things move, lift, stop, or change direction.

The Lever—A Simple Machine

Think about how the lever helped Sonia lift the lid of the paint can.

Simple machines, like the lever, make work much easier. They make a small push or pull into a much bigger one. Simple machines don't need electricity or batteries. You make them work with your muscles.

A bottle opener and a grocery cart are both simple machines.

The Parts of a Lever

A lever has two parts. One part of the lever is a strong bar. This is called the **lever arm**.

The other part of the lever is where the bar rests or sits. This is called the **fulcrum**. The fulcrum lets the lever arm move or turn.

The object that is being moved by the lever is called the **load**.

One lever that you've probably seen is the seesaw. Look at the diagram to find each part of the seesaw lever.

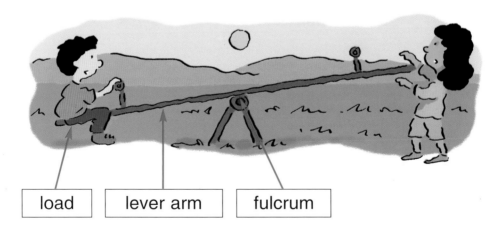

| load | lever arm | fulcrum |

Sonia used a lever to open the paint can. This labeled photograph shows each part of her lever at work.

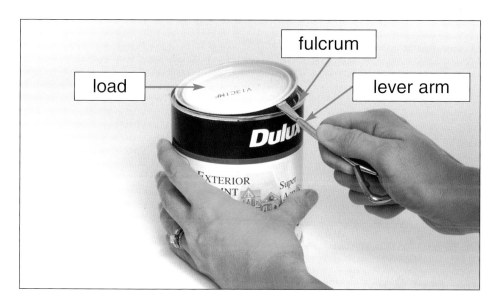

Sonia used her muscles to make the simple machine work. The lever let her lift the lid that was sealed tight on the can. When she pushed down on the lever, the lever turned her pushing force into a strong lifting force. The can opened!

Sonia Has Another Problem

Sonia and her friend Chris are playing on the seesaw.

Sonia's dad wants to try out the seesaw, too, but her dad is much heavier than Chris. Will Sonia be able to lift her dad? How can Sonia lift this heavy load?

An Experiment

How can Sonia use the lever to lift her dad? Try this experiment to see if you can solve Sonia's problem.

What you need

- 6 pencils
- sticky tape
- a ruler
- 5 small, interlocking blocks

What you do

1. Tape 6 pencils together to make a triangle shape.

2. Balance a ruler on top of the pencils.

3. Tape 1 block to one end of the ruler. Place 2 blocks at the other end of the ruler. Note what happens.

4. Move the 2 blocks 2 cm, or 0.8 in, toward the fulcrum (the pencils). What happens?

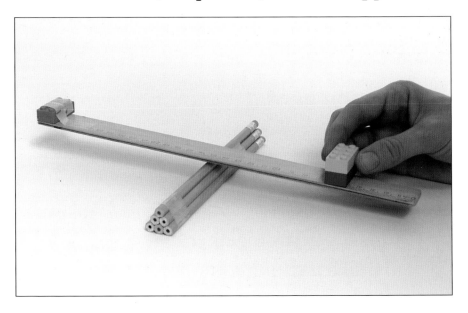

5. Slowly move the 2 blocks farther along the ruler toward the fulcrum. What happens? At what point do the 1 block and the 2 blocks make the ruler balance?

6. Repeat the experiment with 3 blocks, and then 4 blocks. Keep one block taped to one end.

Make a chart like this one to record your results.

Using a Lever to Lift a Load	
Number of blocks in the load	Where I placed the load on the ruler to make it balance
2 blocks	
3 blocks	
4 blocks	

What Did You Find Out?

When you added more blocks, you had a heavier load to lift.

What did you have to do to the load to make the ruler balance?

How a Lever Works

With a lever, you can lift or move something much more easily than without one. In the experiment, the one block pushed down on the lever arm. It created a **force**. A force is either a push or a pull. The lever can make a small force into a bigger force.

In the experiment, you saw this when two, three, or four blocks were lifted with the **effort** of a single block. The effort is the amount of force needed to lift an object.

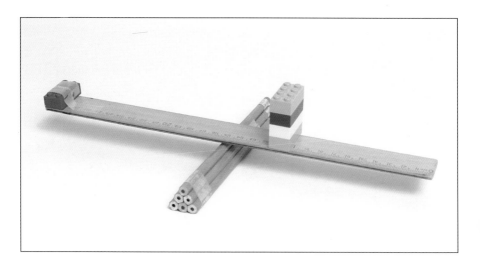

How Can Sonia Lift Her Dad?

Have you figured out how Sonia can lift her dad on the seesaw?

When Sonia goes on the seesaw with her dad, she needs to change his position on the lever arm. Remember how you could lift more with the one block when you changed the position of the two, three, or four blocks?

Here you can see that the distance between the fulcrum and Sonia is greater than the distance between the fulcrum and her dad. Now Sonia can lift her dad.

fulcrum

Levers All Around Us

Levers are everywhere. All the things on these two pages are levers.

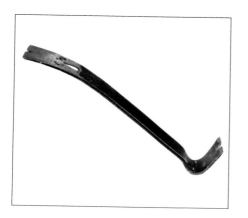

Can you name all the levers? How does each lever make work easier?

Levers in Action

Did you know that scissors, nutcrackers, pliers, and nail clippers are all levers?

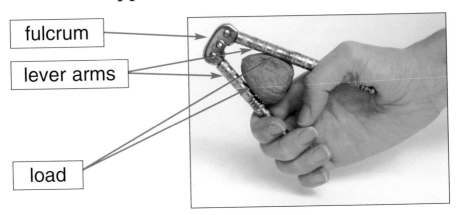

fulcrum

lever arms

load

A nutcracker has two lever arms joined at the fulcrum. The nutcracker pushes against the nut and cracks the shell. This time, the load is not something that is being lifted. The load is the resistance the nut shell has to being cracked.

Try cracking a hard nut first with your bare hands and then with a nutcracker, and you'll see how this machine makes your work easier.

Scissors have two lever arms and are joined at the fulcrum. Look at your scissors to see how they are joined. Notice that the two lever arms can be moved.

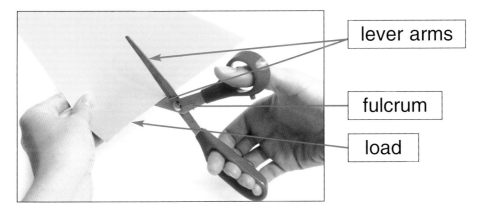

lever arms

fulcrum

load

Levers that have two lever arms that are joined are called **compound levers**. Think of compound levers as you would a compound word. A compound word is two words put together. A compound lever is two lever arms joined together at the fulcrum.

Look again at the pictures on pages 16 and 17. Which levers are compound levers?

Levers in History

The lever has been used for a very long time. A catapult is a lever that was used hundreds of years ago as a weapon. An army attacking an enemy fort or castle would place large stones in a bucket at the end of the catapult's lever arm. The catapult lever was then used to hurl the stones at the enemy fort.

Levers in Space

The Canadarm is used on space shuttles.
It is a robot made up of a series of levers.
Astronauts use the Canadarm to move
satellites in and out of the space station's
loading bay.

Other Simple Machines

Remember, simple machines work with your muscles. A lever is one kind of simple machine. There are others that make it easier to move and lift things.

Lever

Wheel
and Axle

Wedge

Inclined Plane
or Ramp

Pulley

Screw

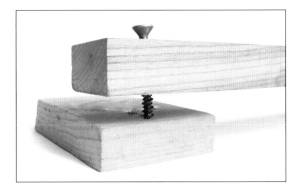

Glossary

catapult a weapon from the past that used a lever to throw stones

compound levers levers that have two lever arms (for example, scissors)

effort the force needed to move something

force a push or pull that changes the position of an object

fulcrum the point on which the lever arm moves

lever arm the bar that rests on the fulcrum

load something that is lifted or moved

simple machines tools that make work easier, using only muscle power

Questions

1. What are the parts of a lever called?
2. What did the experiment with the blocks and the ruler show you?
3. How would you describe a lever and what it does, in your own words?
4. How many simple machines did you use today?